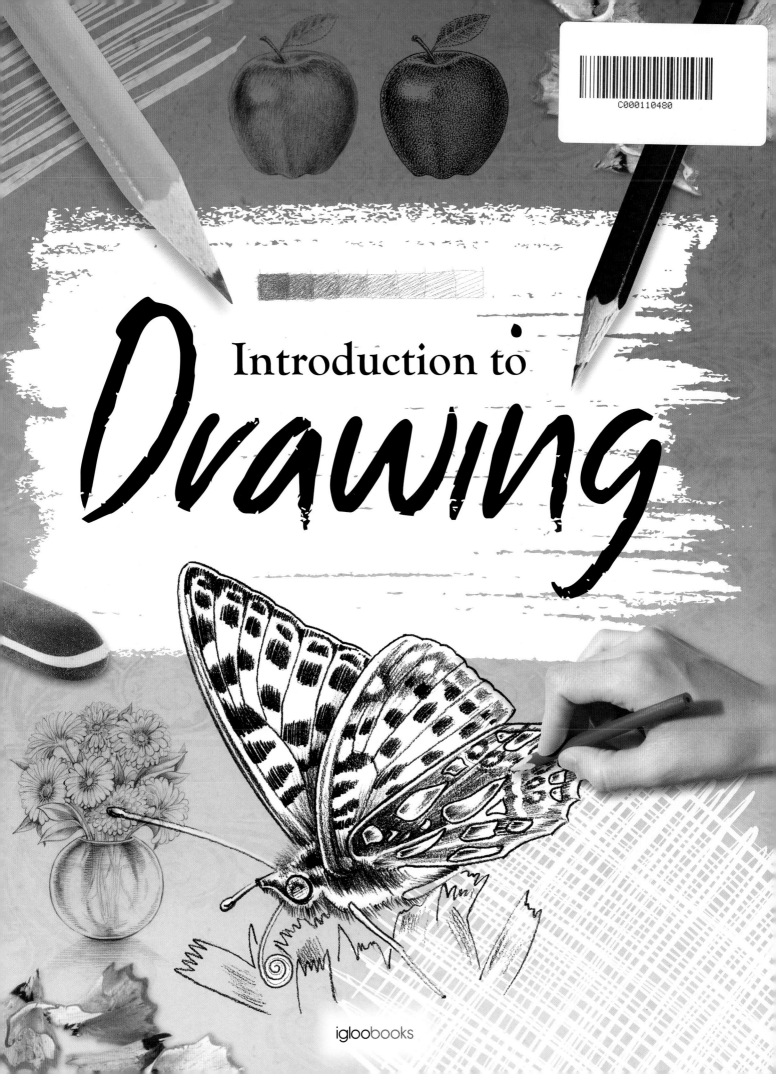

Introduction to Drawing

igloobooks

igloobooks

Published in 2015
by Igloo Books Ltd
Cottage Farm
Sywell
NN6 0BJ
www.igloobooks.com

Cover images © Thinkstock / Getty Images

LEO002 0715
2 4 6 8 10 9 7 5 3 1
ISBN 978-1-78440-286-0

Printed and manufactured in China

Introduction to Drawing

Contents

Introduction

Art is all around us. It is in the beautiful painting that hangs on the wall and it is in the design of our new clothes and shoes. Art can be something aesthetically pleasing such as a striking sculpture or drawing, or it can be something as functional as the chair on which you are sitting.

Elements of art

All art, whether it is functional or designed to evoke a particular emotional reaction, contains certain elements. These elements of art are the building blocks that artists use and without them, art would not be possible. They are:

- Line: a line is a continuous mark that is made on a surface by a moving point. Without line, we would not be able to draw shapes, objects or symbols – art would be impossible.

- Shape: this is an object that has only two dimensions: length and width. Geometric shapes such as circles, rectangles, squares, triangles and so on, have clear edges, while organic shapes have natural, less defined edges.

- Form: this is a three-dimensional object. Sculpture, by its nature, works with forms but those artists who draw or paint in two dimensions, seek to give their art the third dimension – depth.

- Space: this refers to distances or areas around, between or within the components of a piece. Space can be positive (white or light) or negative (black or dark), open or closed, shallow or deep and two-dimensional or three-dimensional. Sometimes space isn't actually within a piece, but the illusion of it is.

- Texture: this is used to describe the way a three-dimensional work feels when touched, or the visual 'feel' of a two-dimensional work.

- Value: this refers to the lightness or darkness of a colour. This is a crucial element when drawing in pencil because you need to use the grey of the pencil to create light and dark values.

- Colour: colour is used to give a drawing more vibrancy. It can also give a drawing the feeling of warmth and contrast.

Using these elements to draw

The aim of this book is to help you to feel confident to draw, whether it's to create something visually appealing that gives pleasure or something that can be used as a starting block to create something else. This book will teach you how to use the elements outlined opposite in your drawings, and how by using them, your drawing skills and confidence will improve.

Getting Started

This chapter contains everything you need to know before you start to draw. You can find out what materials you will need and even how to use them. There is also a wealth of information on basic drawing skills, composition and perspective. This is the perfect introduction to drawing!

Setting Up

While this book has all the information and exercises to help you start drawing, there are a few things you need to think about before you begin. This includes buying your equipment, setting up a studio and going outdoors.

Setting up a studio

There are tips later on in this book for setting up a studio or drawing space, but this is something you need to think about before you start, too. You will need somewhere quiet to draw, or at least somewhere free from distractions. Paying rent on a studio is an expensive commitment, so it's probably a good idea to find somewhere in your house that will be suitable. Set up boundaries if you share your house with other people, so they know that the area is your drawing space.

Buying equipment

By browsing art supply shops, you will see that not only is there a vast range of supplies available to buy, but there is a great disparity in price between them. Usually, less expensive materials and tools are of a lesser quality. They're fine to buy if you want to see if drawing is for you, but you might be better off making an initial investment and buying better quality products to start with. You can also buy materials online, but in doing this, there are no sales assistants to help you to choose the most suitable products. It's a good idea to go into a shop initially and then, once you are familiar with the materials, source them online. When you are starting out, see if you can borrow the larger equipment, such as an easel or tilted worktop, because they are costly investments to make if you're on a tight budget.

Going outdoors

While you can draw indoors, drawing outside can be a wonderful experience. Obviously you need to have suitable weather to do this – the last thing you want is your drawing being soaked by the rain or ripped by the wind! You'll need paper and pencils, plus something to sit on. While you can use any sized paper to draw on, for outdoor sketching, a smaller pad may be more convenient. A pad will also keep the pages together more easily than individual sheets. Store your pencils in some kind of pencil case, in which you can also pack your eraser and a craft knife to sharpen the lead. Take note of where you intend to draw as pencil sharpeners may be better than a sharp-bladed knife.

Artists' Materials

To draw, artists use a wide variety of materials. Some, such as pencils, pastels and charcoal are erasable and so somewhat more forgiving: mistakes can simply be 'wiped out'. Other materials, such as ink, chisel-tipped pens and brush pens are permanent and mistakes are harder to rectify.

Graphite pencils

Graphite pencils are available with hard, medium or soft leads. In most countries, the HB grading system is used to determine the hardness (H) or blackness (B) of the pencil. In this system, 10H is the hardest, while a 10B is the softest. In the United States, pencils are numbered: a #1 is equivalent to a B, #2 an HB, #3 an H and #4, a 2H.

Coloured pencils

Today, coloured pencils are becoming increasingly popular among artists. They are very versatile, especially those that are water soluble, which means they can be used with water. Artists use these pencils to draw their subject but then add water with a brush to soften the hard outlines and blend the colours.

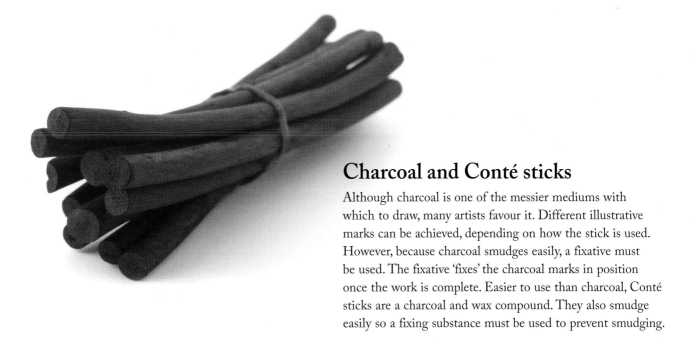

Charcoal and Conté sticks

Although charcoal is one of the messier mediums with which to draw, many artists favour it. Different illustrative marks can be achieved, depending on how the stick is used. However, because charcoal smudges easily, a fixative must be used. The fixative 'fixes' the charcoal marks in position once the work is complete. Easier to use than charcoal, Conté sticks are a charcoal and wax compound. They also smudge easily so a fixing substance must be used to prevent smudging.

Pastels

Like pencils, pastels can be divided into hard and soft types. Hard pastels come in the form of compressed sticks, while soft pastels are usually chunky and crumbly. The particular appeal of soft pastels is their rich, dense colour, which is hard to achieve with other drawing materials.

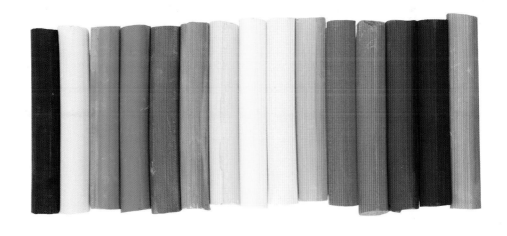

Pens

Pens are often categorised by the type of tip or nib that they have. While felt-tipped pens and fineliners are the most commonly used by artists, chisel-tipped pens now come in a wide range of colours and are becoming more and more popular with artists. With their flexible tip, brush pens can be used to create vibrant, colour-rich drawings.

Artists' Tools

In addition to artists' materials, such as pens, pencils and charcoal sticks, you will need some tools. These include the correct type of paper for the material you are using, erasers, sharpeners and fixing spray.

Paper

Artists' materials that are erasable, such as pencils and charcoal, are often referred to as 'dry', while those that are permanent, including pens and felt tips, are called 'wet'. To make the most of your drawing, you will need to choose the correct type of paper for your material. Dry materials do not work particularly well on smooth paper because they need something on which to grip. Grainier paper adds texture and character to your finished artwork. For pencil drawings, look for paper marked as such. Often this will come in a sketchpad. If your chosen material falls in the 'wet' group, you will need a smooth paper. By using a smoother paper you'll ensure that the grain of the paper doesn't interfere with or catch onto your pen as you draw.

Pencil sharpeners

You will need to keep your pencils sharp. To do this, you can use an ordinary pencil sharpener but make sure you are able to sharpen a long shaft of graphite. This may be more easily achieved by using a craft knife. Craft knives allow you to shave the tip of the pencil to create not only a sharp point, but also to bare more graphite, making the pencil ideal for shading.

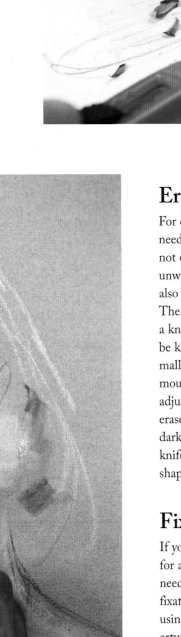

Erasers

For dry materials, you will also need erasers. These are used not only to remove and correct unwanted lines, but they are also used to create highlights. The most versatile eraser is a kneadable eraser. This can be kneaded so that it's quite malleable and can then be moulded into a point to make adjustments. A plastic or vinyl eraser will rub out even the darkest graphite. Keep a craft knife and sandpaper handy to shape your eraser.

Fixing sprays

If you intend to keep your artwork for any length of time, you will need to 'fix' it in place, using a fixative. While some people suggest using hair lacquer, if you want your artwork to last, don't economise on your fixing spray. Look for spray that is specifically suited to the material that you're using. For pencil artwork, you can use any marked 'archival', 'matte finish' or even those marked for pastels and charcoal.

Finding a Workstation

One of the great things about drawing is that you can do it wherever and whenever you like. However, drawing and completing a piece takes considerable time, so you need to ensure you are comfortable as you work. Setting up a work area is very important.

Choosing a work area

Wherever you decide your workstation will be, pay careful attention to your surroundings. Your work area should be a place that inspires creativity – avoid noisy areas, such as the middle of your kitchen or general living areas. Choose somewhere peaceful and calm and that does not have distractions such as a ringing telephone or loud television.

Tables and chairs

Your chair needs to be comfortable. Try to find a height-adjustable chair so that you are able to sit properly and correctly while you draw. A chair with wheels is useful because you can move backwards and forwards easily if you need to. A drafting table is an adjustable worktop with a slanted top. They are great if you aim to draw extensively and are serious about your craft, but can be an expensive investment if you're just starting out. You could improvise and create your own sloping surface by propping up a piece of wood with some books. Creating a slanted worktop is important – if you work on a flat surface, the top will be further away from you than the bottom, and your drawing could be out of proportion.

Light

Good light is essential for good art. You need to be able to see your art clearly and without your eyes becoming sore or tired. If it's possible, try to set up your workstation near a window that offers natural light during the day. You'll need to be near an artificial light source on dull or overcast days and at night, but stay away from fluorescent lights because they can cause headaches. You will probably also need a study lamp with a flexible neck to focus light on your drawings.

Storing and displaying

You will also need somewhere to store your materials. A cart on wheels will keep all your paper, pencils and other drawing equipment neat and tidy until you need it again. You'll need drawers or folders in which to keep your art: stashing them under a rug or bed is not a good idea! To display your art, you can peg them onto a board or an easel. It can be inspirational to easily see your finished art and show off your pieces.

Techniques for Drawing Well

Drawing can be time consuming and, like any activity in which you sit in the same position
for a long time, it can lead to aching muscles and headaches. To help alleviate these symptoms,
you need to sit properly and hold your pencil or other drawing material comfortably and correctly.

Perfect posture

Comfort is crucial – if you're uncomfortable or in a painful sitting position,
your art will suffer for it. Keep your body straight but slightly inclined forward.
If you can, adjust the height of your chair so that your feet are flat on the
floor, or on a footstool, with your knees bent at right angles.

If you're sitting properly and your table is set up correctly, you should be able
to see your drawing without bending your lower back. Try to keep your eyes at a
good distance from your work. If you're too close to your work, you won't be able
to see it properly. Once you're sitting properly, make sure that you take regular
breaks to stretch your muscles.

Scribe's grip

How do you hold your pencil?
Most beginners will hold their
pencil in a scribe's grip. This is
the grip you were probably taught
to use when writing. The problem
with this grip is that writing and
drawing are very different activities.
Writing uses the fingers and wrist
while the whole arm, including the
shoulder, are used for drawing.

Pen grip

Instead of using the scribe's grip, try to draw using the pen grip. To do this, hold your pen or pencil as you would a pen to write, but move your fingers much further from the tip. This grip will give you more control when drawing smaller features, but it is not ideal for working with the side of your pencil or for creating broad strokes. For this, you need to use a violin bow grip.

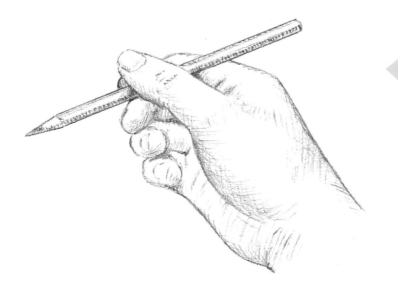

Violin bow grip

To achieve a violin bow grip, hold your pencil with the thumb against all four fingers. This grip will take the control away from your fingers and move it to your wrist and arm at the shoulder.

Sketching Basic Shapes

All objects, from vases and flowers to horses and dogs, can be broken down into a few basic shapes. If you are able to see these basic shapes in everything you draw, you'll be amazed at how easily the rest of the drawing follows.

What shapes?

The basic shapes to look for are squares, rectangles, triangles, cones, cylinders, circles and ovals. Remember, the shapes that you create don't have to be perfectly drawn. Sometimes, an oval may be a little squashed and triangles can look very different, depending on the size of the angles and the lengths of the sides.

Head

To draw the perfect horse, start by drawing your grid. Look at the shape of the horse's head. What shapes can you see? Draw these shapes.

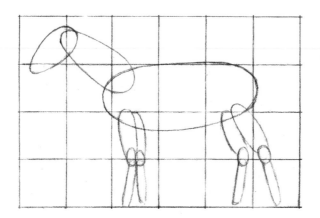

Body

Now you can begin to draw the basic shapes of the horse's body and legs. Notice how the horse's legs aren't just one shape, there is a joint in the middle, and the top of the leg is wider than at the bottom.

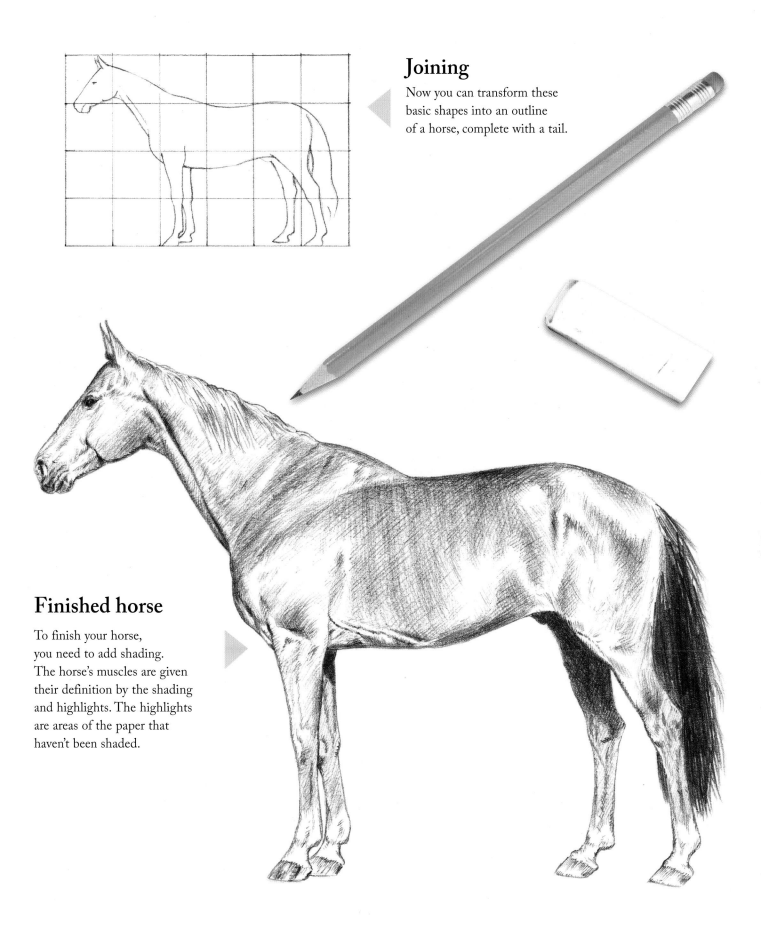

Joining

Now you can transform these basic shapes into an outline of a horse, complete with a tail.

Finished horse

To finish your horse, you need to add shading. The horse's muscles are given their definition by the shading and highlights. The highlights are areas of the paper that haven't been shaded.

Drawing Ellipses

Look at a plate from overhead. Can you see that it is a circle? Now look at the same plate from a sitting position. The shape you see now is an ellipse. Ellipses are circles drawn at an angle or in perspective. They are the curves you see at the rim of rounded objects such as cups, glasses and vases.

How to draw an ellipse

When you draw an ellipse, the two sides should be symmetrical, both vertically and horizontally. The ellipse should be vertical at the left and right points and horizontal at the top and bottom points. To check the symmetry of your ellipse, hold your drawing against a mirror or turn it upside down.

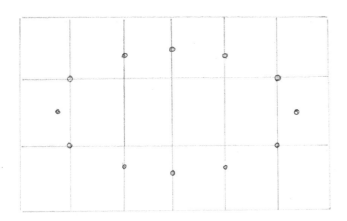

Step 1

There are several ways that you can draw an ellipse, this is our artist's preferred method. To start with, draw a grid. Now mark two dots in the middle of your grid at the same distance from the top and bottom lines, then mark off two dots at the same distance from either side. Add two more dots between each of these four dots.

Step 2

Check the symmetry of your ellipse by drawing a vertical line at each end. Use a ruler to do this.

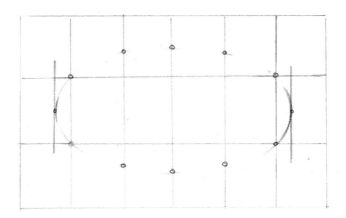

Step 3

Now you can join the dots! Use a steady hand to do this so that you create a smooth shape.

Step 4

To finish your ellipse, rub out the lines of the grid and the dots that you drew in the first step.

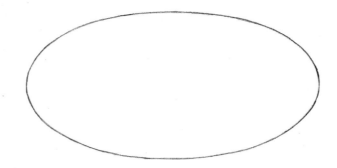

Tone

Sometimes referred to as value or shading, tone is the measure of light and dark in a drawing. Tones range from white through to grey and on to a very dark black. They give your artwork the illusion of depth, thus making it appear three-dimensional and 'lifting' it off the page.

Finding the light

In order to accurately capture the tones of a drawing, you will need to understand light because light will show you where to shade and how much shading is needed. Light can come from a natural light source, such as the sun shining through a window, or an artificial light source, such as a lamp that has been set up near a still life table.

The part of an object closest to the light source is usually the brightest and lightest. These bright areas are called the highlights. Highlights can be created by leaving the white of the paper to show through or by using a kneadable eraser to remove shading. Closest to the highlights, are the lighter tones. The objects further from the light source are the medium and then the darkest tones. These will need darker shading. A cast shadow is a dark section on an adjacent surface that receives little or no light. These shadows are darkest next to the object and lighter as you move away.

Picking your pencils

Different pencils create lighter
and darker shading. A 2H pencil
will give a lighter tone while a 6B
pencil will create a very dark shade.
You could also use the same pencil
and apply different amounts of
pressure when holding it. If using
this method, always begin with
light, loose strokes, and increase
the pressure to produce darker tones.

Layering up

The density of shading used will also affect the tone – the denser
the shading, the darker the tone. However, repeatedly shading in
the same direction can give art a 'blocky' look. To smooth out
the tone, rub gently over your drawing in a light circular motion
with your fingertip. This will give your art a smoother finish.

Hatching and Cross-hatching

Shading can be created in several ways. These include hatching and cross-hatching.
You can use one method in a drawing or a combination of both, depending on your
subject and your personal preference.

Hatching

Hatching is probably the most widely used method of
shading. This involves drawing straight or curved lines
next to, or parallel to, each other. These lines are called
a set, and they can be close together or further apart,
depending on the effect you wish to achieve. For lighter
tones, the lines need to be far apart but for darker tones,
they should be closer together.

Cross-hatching

Cross-hatching allows for a smoother transition of values. Here, one set of lines is drawn at a right angle to another set so that the lines overlap. The smaller the gap between the lines, the denser the shading or darker the tone. Cross-hatching is especially useful for ink drawings because artists cannot make the ink lighter or darker.

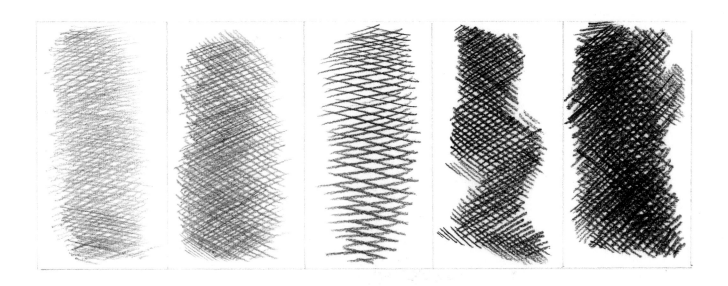

Creating Texture

Smooth, rough, spiky, furry and bumpy are just some of the textures that artists recreate to achieve a tactile quality in their drawings. This gives the work the illusion of a surface. By adjusting the tones of a drawing, artists can create different textures. Hatching and cross-hatching, loops and squiggles and pointillism are just some of the techniques you can use.

Hatching and cross-hatching

As well as using hatching and cross-hatching to add tone to a drawing, you can use them to add texture. These two techniques are usually used to create a smoother, more muted texture.

Loops and squiggles

To create a softer texture, artists use a combination of loops and squiggles. When these are closer together, the texture looks smoother than when the loops and squiggles are further apart.

Pointillism

Using dots to create a pattern or texture is called pointillism. This technique works well on lighter shaded areas. The more dots you use, the more textured the surface.

Paper

While you will need to use a rougher paper for your graphite to stick to the surface, different papers will create different textures. If you use paper with a rougher surface, your final drawing will be rougher.

Dents and holes

You can also use different objects to create dents and holes to give different surfaces. Any tool that makes a mark, from an eraser to a thick, blunt needle, can be used to add texture to your drawing.

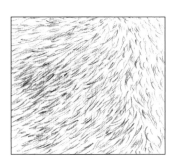

Fur

To create a furry texture, use a combination of short and long lines in the same direction as the fur grows.

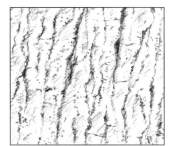

Bark of tree

Broken, uneven lines with varying spaces between give the illusion of a rough bark.

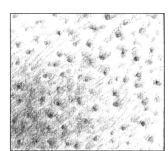

Orange peel

As well as smoothness, orange peel has dimples that need to be captured.

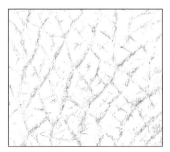

Skin

If you look closely at your skin, you will see that it isn't smooth, but rather has a mesh-like appearance.

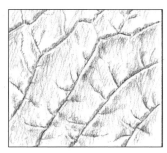

Leaves

The veins of a leaf need to be drawn darker than the background.

Hair

Because hair is similar to fur, you can use a similar technique to the one used to draw fur.

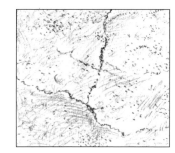

Fabric

Use cross-hatching with the lines slightly apart to create the illusion of fabric.

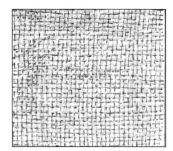

Brick

The surface of a brick has cracks and lines in it that you can capture using shading.

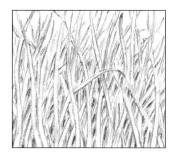

Grass

The bottom of the grass is denser so it is shown by using darker tones than the top of the blades.

Snake skin

By shading the edges of each diamond shape darker, the scales are given depth.

Using a Grid

A grid is like an artist's safety net because, instead of focusing on an entire picture, a grid allows you to work on a drawing square by square. Grids are especially useful when creating still life pieces or when drawing from photographs.

What is a grid?

A grid is a piece of cardboard or acetate with horizontal and vertical lines drawn on it to create squares. Grids can be made up of any number of squares, but all the squares must be equal in size. When using a cardboard grid, an artist places it behind the object or collection of objects he or she is drawing. An acetate or plastic grid can be placed over the photograph that is being copied. The artist then plots the same number of equal-sized squares on his or her paper. Any part of the object's outline that falls into a certain square on the big grid is drawn on the corresponding square on the artist's sheet of paper.

How to use a grid

Step 1: measure the height and width of the object in the photograph. Use these measurements to draw a grid of even squares onto a sheet of acetate.

Step 2: place the grid behind or over your photograph so that the entire object is in the grid. Secure the grid.

Step 3: draw a corresponding grid on your sheet of paper. It must have exactly the same number of rows and columns as the acetate grid.

Step 4: draw the subject square by square so that it matches the photograph.

Step 5: erase the grid.

Step 1

Once you have drawn the grid over your photograph, draw a grid with the same number of squares on your paper. Now draw the basic shapes that you can see.

Step 2

Now add more detail to your car's basic shape so that it starts to look like a car.

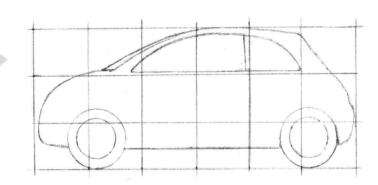

Step 3

Now you can add the values to give the car its three-dimensional shape. The tyres are the darkest because they are made from rubber and the inside of the car is in shadow so that, too, will need to be darker. The bodywork is metallic so there are lots of highlights. By shading underneath the car, the car is grounded.

Composition

Artists position things in their drawings to achieve balance – all the component or individual parts need to work together. This 'balance' is called composition. A well-balanced drawing will captivate the viewer.

Paper shape

One of the most basic aspects of composition is choosing the size and shape of your piece of paper. To use the correct sized paper, everything must fit on the paper but the paper cannot be too large – if it is, the viewer's eyes will not be able to focus on the drawing. The shape of the paper can be landscape or portrait, horizontal or vertical. Again, everything needs to fit on the paper within the chosen size.

Focal point

Focusing on focal points

Once you have chosen the size and shape of your paper, you need to decide where to draw the focal point. The focal point in a drawing is the point to which the viewer's eyes are drawn. The focal point is usually the main subject of a drawing. Sometimes, there are two focal points. The secondary focal point must work with the main focal point to achieve a balance.

Drawing your focal point

If you position your focal point exactly in the centre of your piece of paper, or if you divide your paper in half with a tall object in the middle, your drawing will have very little impact. Similarly, if the same sized objects are placed equidistant on either side of the centre line, your drawing will be rather boring.

To achieve a good balance, one of the most commonly used theories for positioning a focal point is called the 'golden ratio' or 'golden mean'. The golden ratio was discovered by the Greek mathematician, Euclid. He worked out that a sequence of numbers (3, 5, 8, 13, 21…) gave a series of ratios. This means that if a line is drawn by combining two successive numbers in the ratio, for example 5 and 8 to give a line of 13, and divided into the two component lengths (one of 5 and one of 8), the ratio of the smaller part (5) to the larger part (8) is the same as the ratio of the larger part (8) to the whole (13). So:

'C' (A+B) is to 'A' as 'A' is to 'B'

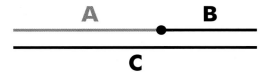

If you divide your paper up according to the golden ratio, where the vertical and horizontal lines of the ratio intersect (usually a third of the way in and a third of the way up or down), you will find one of the better places to position your focal point. Once you know where to draw it, you need to make the focal point stand out. This can be done by using more detailed shading or by adding darker values. The focal point should also be the largest item in the drawing.

Proportion

Proportion is the relationship between the size, location, or amount of one element of the whole to another element of the whole. Good proportion adds balance and harmony to a drawing. However, it is often easier to pinpoint something that is out of proportion than something that is in proportion.

Standard proportion

The correct height, width and depth of an object compared to its surroundings is called standard proportion. One of the best examples of standard proportion is found on the human body, in particular the human face. All faces are roughly oval. The width of the oval is approximately five eyes wide. The eyes are positioned about halfway down the oval. The bottom of the nose is as wide as the gap between the inner corners of the eyes. The pupils of the eyes usually line up with the corners of the mouth. A person's ears are found between the eye line and the imaginary line drawn at the bottom of the nose, the 'nose line'. By following these guidelines when you draw a face, the face will be in proportion and look balanced.

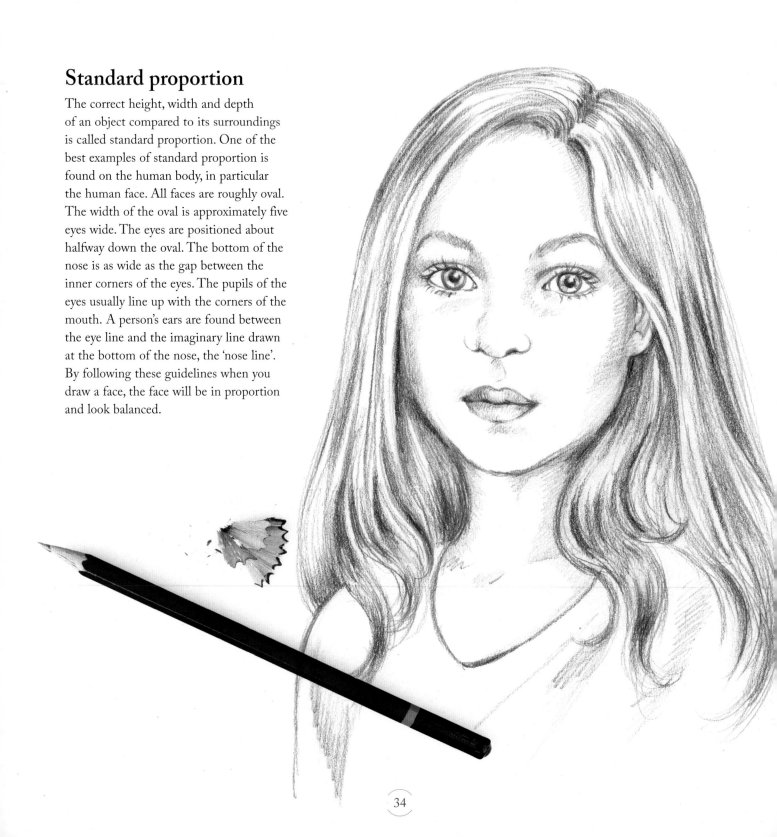

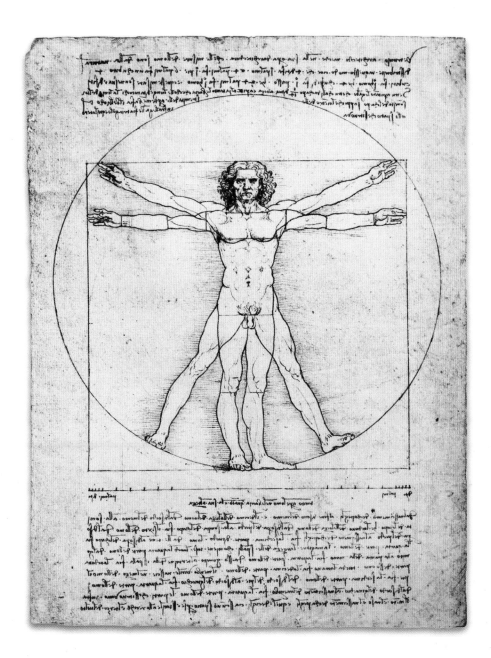

Drawing in proportion

To make sure that you draw your subject, regardless of what it is, in proportion, there are simple steps you can follow. Start by looking for something in your subject that you can measure. For example, an apple in a still life or the length of your subject's head. Once you've worked out the size of this object, measure the rest of your subject in relation to it. This will mean working with ratios, so to make things simple, use ratios that are easy to work with, such as 1:2 and 1:4. Remember when you are measuring, to hold your arm straight and stand at the same point each time. For good measure, check everything twice before you mark your paper and then check again after you've marked your paper – if something's not right, re-measure until it is!

Cropping

Cropping is a technique that involves a truncation, or cutting off, of some parts of the subject. It brings the viewer closer to the subject of a drawing and creates drama. However, cropping can make it difficult to balance a drawing.

Cropping and composition

As discussed earlier, when you're beginning a new drawing, you need to look at the size and shape of the subject and choose your paper size accordingly. You know now that to achieve a good composition and balance in your art, the focal point should ideally be on the 'golden mean' and by dividing your paper accordingly, you can work out where this is. However, if there is a lot of white space or unwanted objects around your focal point, you may want to crop these so that you guide your viewer's eye to the focal point. By cropping out the white space or unwanted objects, you will bring the viewer closer to the subject, but will your drawing still look balanced?

Judging composition

One of the best ways to judge whether a drawing is balanced or not is to complete a thumbnail sketch in which you draw your subject as you'd like to crop it. Then, stand back a little and look at your drawing. If you feel your paper looks too crowded, it is likely that you've cropped too closely. If you've cropped too closely, your subject may also be losing its shape or some of the values or tones that define it. If your subject grabs your attention and lures you into the drawing, you've cropped successfully.

To the edge

Another way to crop your drawing and focus on the subject, is to let part of your drawing run to one or more of the paper's edges. This will change the composition of your drawing. Depending on the subject, it may also result in a triangular composition that does not work for your subject. Again, stand back and evaluate the balance and composition.

Using a Viewfinder

A viewfinder is an adjustable frame that enables you to see the subject of your drawing from various viewpoints. You can use a viewfinder to plan any composition, whether you are drawing from a photograph, a section of your garden or a still life that you've set up.

Make a viewfinder

Viewfinders are readily available at good art shops, but if you don't want to buy a viewfinder, you can easily make your own. To do this, you will need a large sheet of neutral-coloured cardboard. Neutral card is the best choice because a brightly coloured card may detract from the subject of your drawing. Using a ruler, measure two 'L' shapes exactly the same size. Cut out the shapes using a sharp craft knife and ruler. It will be useful to make a selection of different-sized viewfinders – you can use smaller ones for working from photographs and larger ones for working outdoors.

Using your viewfinder

Once you've decided on the subject of your artwork, place one 'L' over the other to create either a square or rectangular viewfinder. Now slide both 'L's to adjust the size and shape of your view through the viewfinder. When you find a suitable composition, use tape or paper clips to hold the frame together. Larger viewfinders will need to be anchored so that you have two free hands with which to draw. You can do this by cutting out a section from a Styrofoam cup and slotting the viewfinder into it. The image you see through the viewfinder is the image you will draw. If you are drawing from a photograph, you can mark the inside four corners of the viewfinder on your photograph so that you know what you need to draw.

View through a window

When drawing landscapes, instead of using cardboard frames to make a viewfinder, you can use windows and doors to create an interesting view. This means that instead of trying to draw an entire garden, you can look through the window and draw just the area that you see.

Drawing with a viewfinder

When drawing while using a viewfinder, it is very important to keep your head, the viewfinder, and the subject of your drawing all exactly the same distances and in the same places while you draw. If things move, the proportions of your drawing will change, quite possibly without you realising it.

Measuring Angles

As students, most people would have used a protractor to measure angles as part of a lesson in mathematics. At the time, this skill may have seemed very irrelevant, but measuring angles is a vital skill to render accurate drawings.

Drawing precisely

When you measure angles, you need to do this methodically so that your measurements are as accurate as possible. Each time you measure a part of your subject, stand or sit in exactly the same place and at the same height. In the same way you worked with proportion, measure at least twice before you mark your paper.

Protractors

To use a protractor accurately, find a reference line against which you can measure your angles. Hold your protractor in front of your image and check the angle of the part of your subject you are measuring. While protractors will give you very precise measurements, other tools and methods you can use may not be as precise, but may be easier to use.

Pencil power

There are two ways you can use pencils to measure
angles. The first method of measurement uses just
one pencil, while for the second method, you'll need
two pencils. If you're using one pencil, find a vertical
line in your subject or behind your subject, such as
a door frame. This is your reference line. Now, tilt
your pencil to align with the feature you are measuring.
Using the horizontal line of your paper, keep your hand
steady as you transfer the measurement to your paper.
If you want to use two pencils to measure angles, hold
them both in the same hand. One pencil should be
vertical while you align the second with the part of
the subject you are measuring. If you find this second
method helpful, you can fashion your own cardboard
measuring tool by taking two strips of cardboard and
joining them together with a split pin.

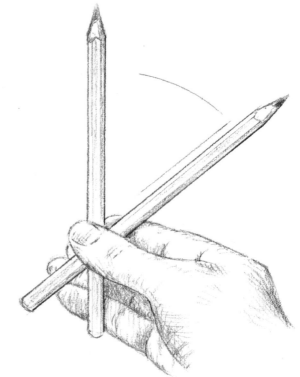

Using circles

Another way to measure
angles is to think of your
subject as having 12 equal
segments, much the same as
the face on an analogue clock.
Measure the angles against the
12 segments. If you're using
a viewfinder already, you can
add crosshairs to it and use
them to measure the angles.

Perspective

One of the challenges of drawing is to create the illusion of three dimensions. Without perspective, this is impossible to do. Perspective is a method of representing subjects and parts of the subject so that they recede in the distance and appear to be further away than they actually are.

Linear perspective

Although sometimes called geometric perspective, linear perspective is usually what people mean when they talk about perspective drawing. Before you can understand perspective, you need to know some basic terminology:

• Horizon line: this is an imaginary horizontal line drawn at eye level. The horizon line divides your line of vision when you look straight ahead of you.

• Vanishing point: this is the point on the horizon line where the straight lines of an object converge and seem to disappear or vanish.

Placing your subject

Where you place your subject in relation to the horizon line in your drawing will have a great effect on the composition of your artwork. For example, if your drawing is at eye level, the viewer will feel as though the drawing is an extension of his or her space, and he or she will view the image in relation to their body. Because the viewer's eye is naturally drawn towards the horizon line, a high eye level will focus more attention on the middle and rear areas of your drawing. A low eye level means that more attention will be focused on the rear area of the drawing, allowing more space to draw the sky. Having a large area of sky can help to create a specific mood in a drawing.

More About Perspective

Linear perspective can be achieved by using either one-point, two-point or three-point perspective. Drawing cubes and boxes will help you to understand how one-point and two-point perspective work in practise.

One-point perspective

In one-point perspective, the frontal face of an object is closest to the viewer and the edges converge and disappear at a single vanishing point.

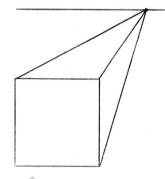

Step 1
Draw a horizon line and mark vanishing point on line. Draw an outline of a square.

Step 2
Draw lines to link the vanishing point and the three corners of the square.

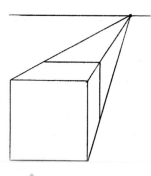

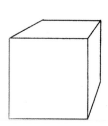

Step 3
Draw horizontal and vertical lines to complete the back of the cube.

Step 4
Use an eraser to rub out the lines so that you are left with a cube.

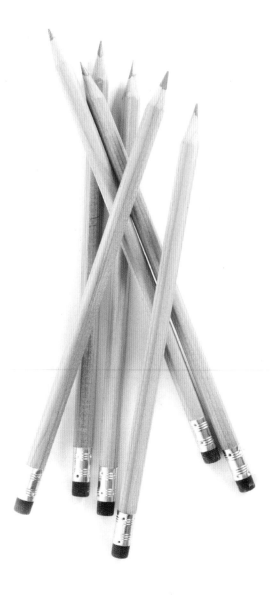

Two-point perspective

In two-point perspective, it will seem as though you are looking at an object or scene from one corner, with two sets of parallel lines moving away from you. Because each set of parallel lines has its own vanishing point, in two-point perspective, there are two vanishing points.

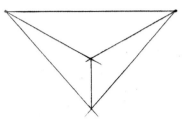 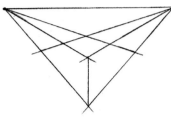 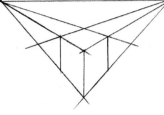

Step 1

Draw a horizon line with vanishing points at both ends of the horizon line. Draw a vertical line in the middle of the horizon line but lower down. Join the vertical line at the top and bottom with the vanishing points.

Step 2

Draw two more diagonal lines that go back to the vanishing points, so that your drawing looks like the one above.

Step 3

Using the lines you drew in step two, draw two vertical lines where the lines intersect. These will be the sides of your box.

Step 4

Use an eraser to rub out the lines so that you are left with your box.

Three-point perspective

Three-point perspective is most often used in drawing buildings and other structures that are viewed from a low or high eye level. If the subject of a drawing is above the horizon line, the viewer will be looking up at it. This will make a building seem tall. Similarly, the viewer will be looking down at the subject if it is drawn below the horizon line. Three-point perspective uses three sets of parallel lines and three vanishing points.

Horizon Line

Vanishing Point

Choosing a subject

By now, you've worked through this book and so you know what perspective is, you can place your subject so that the composition 'works' and you know a 2B from a 4H, but how do you use all this new-found knowledge to draw something? The first thing you need to do is to find a willing subject to draw. Often, this is one of the hardest things about starting out.

Draw your current life

It has always been said that writers should write about what they know. In many ways, the same can be said of artists. This is because if you draw what you know about, your familiarity will fuel your confidence. If you are confident before you start to draw, you will feel bolder with your pencils or charcoal and more inclined to try something new. Knowing your subject will give you an innate knowledge of the finer details that are invaluable to drawing precisely and accurately. However, always drawing what you know about, may lead to boredom, and sometimes you will need a change in subject.

Draw what interests you

For many people, there is something that fascinates them and that they find interesting. If you're interested in something, draw it! Even if it is something that you don't know very well, as long as you find it interesting you will enjoy drawing it. You will, however, need to study it carefully before you start to draw it.

Draw what is around you

Many people are surrounded by subjects worthy of drawing without even realising it. Subjects like your pets, a bowl of fruit that sits on your kitchen counter or a musical instrument make for interesting things to draw. Try to find subjects that are rich or varied in colour, subjects that capture the light in an interesting way or subjects that have unusual angles. If you have a garden, there are undoubtedly many things you could draw, from flowers in bloom to birds and insects that live there.

Know your limits

While there may be many things that inspire you and that you want to draw, it is always worthwhile knowing or acknowledging your abilities. If you tackle something that is incredibly complex and you are just starting out, chances are you'll be put off and frustrated before the drawing is complete. Accept your level and although you should try to improve it with each drawing you do, remember that it's not a race to get there. Practise the basic skills and the more difficult skills will follow.